Program Authors

Peter Afflerbach

Camille Blachowicz

Candy Dawson Boyd

Elena Izquierdo

Connie Juel

Edward Kame'enui

Donald Leu

Jeanne R. Paratore

P. David Pearson

Sam Sebesta

Deborah Simmons

Alfred Tatum

Sharon Vaughn

Susan Watts Taffe

Karen Kring Wixson

Glenview, Illinois • Boston, Massachusetts • Chandler, Arizona •
Upper Saddle River, New Jersey

We dedicate Reading Street to
Peter Jovanovich.

His wisdom, courage,
and passion for education
are an inspiration to us all.

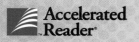
Accelerated Reader®

About the Cover Artist

Daniel Moreton lives in New York City, where he uses his computer to create illustrations for books. When he is not working, Daniel enjoys cooking, watching movies, and traveling. On a trip to Mexico, Daniel was inspired by all of the bright colors around him. He likes to use those colors in his art.

Acknowledgments appear on page 218, which constitute an extension of this copyright page.

ISBN-13: 978-0-328-45556-0
ISBN-10:   0-328-45556-3
4 5 6 7 8 9 10 V042 14 13 12 11

PEARSON

CC1

Reading
STREET

Dear Reader,

Are you enjoying your travels along *Scott Foresman Reading Street?* What new skills have you learned to help you read and understand new things? What strategies have helped you smooth out the "bumps in the road" as you read?

As you continue along *Reading Street,* you will read about people in communities at home, in school, and in neighborhoods. You will also read about communities in nature. So buckle your seat belt and enjoy the trip!

Sincerely,
The Authors

Communities

What is a community?

Week 2

Week 3

Unit 2 Contents

Week 6

Envision It! A Comprehension Handbook

**Envision It! Visual Skills
Handbook EI•1–EI•6**

**Envision It! Visual Strategies
Handbook EI•7–EI•18**

Don Leu
The Internet Guy

Right before our eyes, the nature of reading and learning is changing. The Internet and other technologies create new opportunities, new solutions, and new literacies. New reading comprehension skills are required online. They are increasingly important to our students and our society.

Those of us on the Reading Street team are here to help you on this new, and very exciting, journey.

See It!

- **Big Question Video**

- **Concept Talk Video**

- **Envision It! Animations**

- **eReaders**

- **Interactive Sound-Spelling Cards**

Hear It!

- *Sing with Me* **Animations**

- **eSelections**

- **Grammar Jammer**

- **Vocabulary Activities**

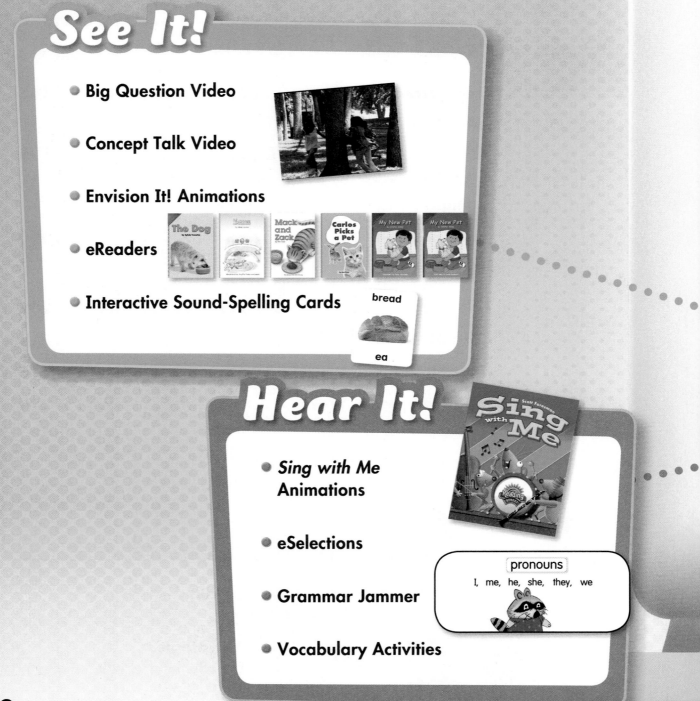

Concept Talk Video

File   Edit   View   Favorites   Tools   Help

http://www.ReadingStreet.com

Do It!

- **Journal Word Bank**

- **Story Sort**

- **Letter Tile Drag and Drop**

- **Online Assessment**

- **Vocabulary Activities**

Communities

What is a community?

Objectives

• Listen closely to speakers and ask questions to help you better understand the topic. • Share information and ideas about the topic. Speak at the correct pace.

Oral Vocabulary

Let's Talk About

People in Communities

- Share ideas about families as communities.

- Take part in a discussion about what a family does together.

READING STREET ONLINE
CONCEPT TALK VIDEO
www.ReadingStreet.com

13

Objectives
● Pick out sounds at the beginning, in the middle, and at the end of one-syllable words. ● Break up one-syllable words into each sound that makes up the word.

Phonemic Awareness

Let's
Listen
for

Sounds

Read Together

● Find three things that begin with the sound /sh/. Say each sound in the words.

● Find something that ends with the sound /sh/. Say the ending sound.

● Find two things that begin with the sound /th/. Say the beginning sound.

● Find three things that rhyme with *tall*. Say the sound in the middle of those words.

READING STREET ONLINE
SOUND-SPELLING CARDS
www.ReadingStreet.com

MOVIE

14

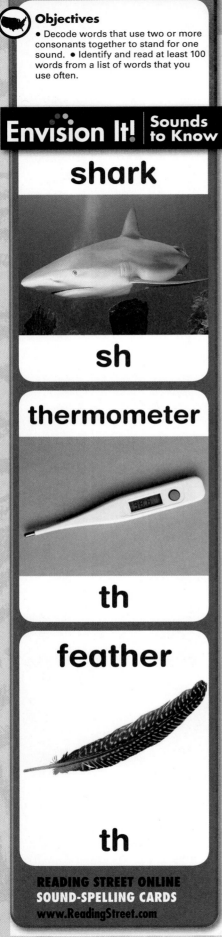

Envision It! | Sounds to Know

shark

sh

thermometer

th

feather

th

Phonics

🔵 Consonant Digraphs *sh, th*

Words I Can Blend

th	i	s

p	a	th

f	i	sh

w	i	th

sh	o	p

Sentences I Can Read

1. This path ends at Black Hill.

2. Can Pen sell fish with us at the shop?

Words I Can Read

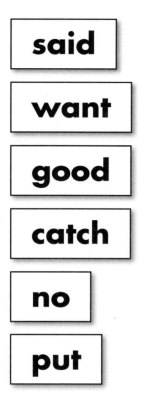

said

want

good

catch

no

put

Sentences I Can Read

1. That man said he did want to catch a good nap.

2. No, Beth can not put that bell on this shelf.

Envision It! | **Sounds to Know**

ball

a

chalk

al

Phonics

🎯 Vowel Sound in *ball: a, al*

Words I Can Blend

Sentences I Can Read

1. All kids must walk in the hall.

2. That tall man can talk with Jan.

Last fall, my math class had a trip to Glen Hill Mall.

Mom said it was good that I went with them. She put cash in my hand and said, "I want a small gift for Max. Can you get it?"

No one can catch a ball like Max. I got a swell mitt for him at this fun shop.

An **animal fantasy** is a story with animals that act like people. Next you will read about Max and Ruby—rabbits that go fishing.

20

Max and Ruby

A Big Fish for Max

written and designed by

Rosemary Wells

illustrated

by Jody Wheeler

Question of the Week

What does a family do together?

"I wish I had a fish to eat," said Max.

"Then we will catch a big fish,"
said Grandma.

"We can walk to the park," said Ruby.

"And Max will catch a big fish."

"Good," said Max. "Yum, yum, yum!"

The path in the park led to the pond.

"Max can fish in this pond," said Ruby.

Max sat.

He got a red ball in his net.

But no fish bit.

Then Max got a black ship in his net.
But no fish bit.

And then Max got a clam shell
in his net.

"I want to call the fish," said Ruby.
"Then I can talk to the fish."
But still no fish bit.

"Well, we can all walk to the fish
shop," said Grandma.
"And we can talk to the fish man."

The fish man had lots of fish in a box.
"We want a fresh fish," said Grandma.
"That fat fish is good."

At home, Grandma put the fish
in a hot pan.
Then Ruby put the fish in a dish.

"Yum, yum, yum!" said Max.

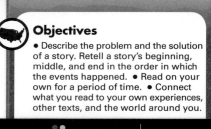
Envision It! Retell

READING STREET ONLINE
STORY SORT
www.ReadingStreet.com

34

Think Critically

1. Max, Ruby, and Grandma care about each other. How do you show you care for others? Text to Self

2. Was this story funny or serious? Why do you think so? Author's Purpose

3. What is the first thing that Max gets in his net? Sequence

4. Did you predict how Max would get a big fish? Was your prediction correct?

   Predict and Set Purpose

5. Look Back and Write Look back at pages 30 and 31. Where does Max get a big fish? Write about it. Use evidence from the story to support your answer.

   TEST PRACTICE Extended Response

Rosemary Wells

Ms. Wells says, "Some of my most pleasurable memories as a child were of fishing with my father. We used to catch snapper blues, and my mother cooked them in parsley and butter that night. Today fish is still one of my favorite things to eat."

When Rosemary Wells writes stories about Max and Ruby, she thinks about what her own two girls said and did when they were children.

Here are other books by Rosemary Wells.

Use the Reading Log in the *Reader's and Writer's Notebook* to record your independent reading.

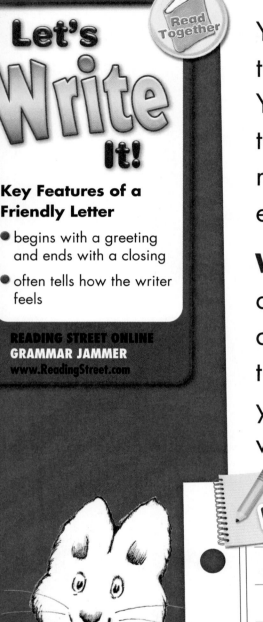

Key Features of a Friendly Letter

● begins with a greeting and ends with a closing

● often tells how the writer feels

READING STREET ONLINE GRAMMAR JAMMER
www.ReadingStreet.com

Friendly Letter

You write a **friendly letter** to someone you know well. You can tell the person things about you. The student model on the next page is an example of a friendly letter.

Writing Prompt Think about things your family does together. Write a letter to persuade someone in your family to do something with you.

Writer's Checklist

Remember, you should . . .

☑ start your letter with a friendly greeting.

☑ give the reader reasons to do something with you.

☑ put your sentences in an order that makes sense.

36

Dear Mom,

   I like to walk to the park.

Can you please walk with me?

  We can see trees and birds.

We can ride a boat in the

pond.

   It will be fun.

            Your son,

            Marco

Genre
Friendly
Letter
The letter begins with **Dear Mom.**

This **noun, boat,** names a thing.

Writing Trait
Organization
The sentences are in an order that makes sense.

Conventions

- **Nouns**

  Remember A **noun** names a person, a place, an animal, or a thing.

- The word **man** names a person. **Home** names a place. **Fox** names an animal. **Net** names a thing.

•

Objectives

● Figure out whether a story is true or make-believe and explain why.

Genre
Literary Nonfiction

● Literary nonfiction is narrative text that tells about real people, places, and events. It is told like a story.

● Literary nonfiction can be a biography, or a story about someone's life.

● Literary nonfiction can be an autobiography, or a story about someone's life written by that person.

● As you read "At Home," think about what you know about literary nonfiction.

At Home

Plants use water.
Plants use the sun.
I want to help plants.

Dad puts pots on the shelf.

Let's Think About...

Who do you think is telling us about plants and pots? **Literary Nonfiction**

39

Let's **Think** About...

Do you think this selection is true or a fantasy? Explain why. **Literary Nonfiction**

Mom cuts the grass.

Sis can catch Gus.
We talk and have fun.

Let's **Think** About...

What makes this selection literary nonfiction?
Literary Nonfiction

Let's **Think** About...

Reading Across Texts How are the families in *A Big Fish for Max* and "At Home" alike?

Writing Across Texts Write sentences about what the family in *A Big Fish for Max* likes to do and what the family in "At Home" likes to do.

41

Let's Learn It!

Read Together

READING STREET ONLINE VOCABULARY ACTIVITIES
www.ReadingStreet.com

One of the best days of my life was when I won the big race. First, I stood at the starting line. Next, our coach said, "Go!" I ran as fast as I could. I was the winner!

Get Ready For Grade 2

Use words such as *first, next,* and *last* when speaking.

Listening and Speaking

Relate an Experience in Sequence When we tell about things that happen to us, we use words such as *first, next,* and *last.* When we listen to others, we ask questions if we don't understand.

Practice It! Think of something exciting that happened to you. Tell others what happened first, next, and last. Use nouns to name things.

Vocabulary

A singular **noun** names a person, animal, place, or thing. We can identify and sort nouns into word groups that name people, animals, places, or things.

Practice It! Read these singular nouns. Identify and sort them into the categories of people, animals, places, or things.

fish   **ball**   **shop**   **boy**

Fluency

Accuracy and Rate Read the sentences. Say the word you see. Blend the sounds to read the word. Put the word in the sentence. Ask yourself if it makes sense.

Practice It!

1. That was a good walk.

2. All the fish in the pond want to swim.

3. Jan put small shells in her bag.

Oral Vocabulary

Let's Talk About

Read Together

People in Communities

● Share ideas about schools as communities.

● Share ideas about a classroom community.

READING STREET ONLINE
CONCEPT TALK VIDEO
www.ReadingStreet.com

You've learned **1 0 2** *Amazing Words* so far this year!

4

Objectives
- Say a group of words that rhyme using different groups of letters.
- Tell the difference between long- and short-vowel sounds in words that have one syllable.
- Combine sounds together to say words with one and two syllables.

Let's Listen for

Sounds

- Find three things that rhyme with *take*.

- Find something that rhymes with *tap*. Now change the short *a* sound to a long *a* sound. Say the new word.

- Find two things that rhyme with *space*. Say the sounds in each word.

- Find two things that begin with the sound /j/.

Read Together

**READING STREET ONLINE
SOUND-SPELLING CARDS**
www.ReadingStreet.com

Envision It! | **Sounds to Know**

rake

a_e

READING STREET ONLINE SOUND-SPELLING CARDS
www.ReadingStreet.com

Phonics

Long *a: a_e*

Words I Can Blend

b r a v e

m a d e

t r a d e

w a k e

b a k e

Sentences I Can Read

1. That brave man made him trade.

2. Will Nat wake up and bake it?

48

Words I Can Read

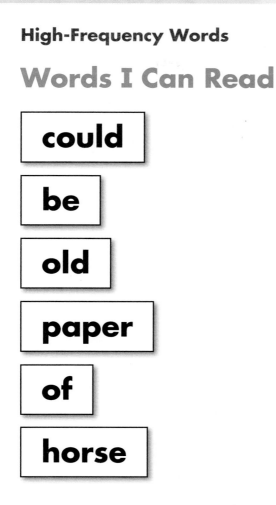

Sentences I Can Read

1. Could it be that this old box is made of paper?

2. Take this black horse and place it in the shade, Jake.

Objectives
- Decode words with consonants.
- Decode words that end in with a silent "e".

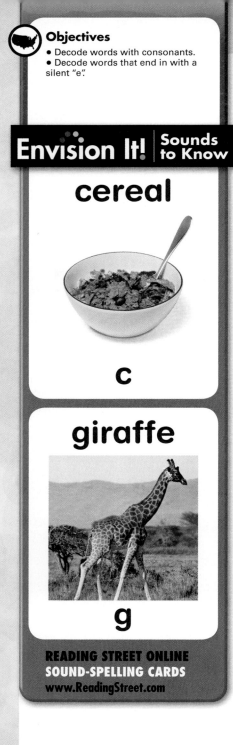

Envision It! | **Sounds to Know**

cereal

c

giraffe

g

READING STREET ONLINE
SOUND-SPELLING CARDS
www.ReadingStreet.com

Phonics

🎯 Consonants
c/s/, g/j/

Words I Can Blend

| r | a | c | e |

| p | a | c | e |

| p | a | g | e |

| g | e | m |

| c | e | n | t | s |

Sentences I Can Read

1. Kate ran that race at a fast pace.

2. Did Dave spot that gem on page one that costs ten cents?

I Can Read!

Gabe saves old stuff. He kept an old pad of paper. Its last page had space for him to trace a face on it.

Gabe asks, "Could this page be a horse mask?"

Mom said, "Get rid of it!"

You've learned

- Long *a*: *a_e*
- Consonants *c/s/*, *g/j/*

High-Frequency Words
could be old
paper of horse

The Farmer in the Hat

by Pat Cummings

Genre

Realistic fiction has characters that act like real people. You will read a story about classmates putting on a play.

Beth

Dave

Grace

Question of the Week

How is a school a community?

Max

Jake

Meg

53

Beth got the hat. "I could be the farmer, Old MacDonald, in this play," said Beth.

"But I am the farmer, Beth," said Dave.

"You can be a pig," said Beth.
"A pig!" Dave made an odd face.

Grace went up on stage. "Let us make paper masks of faces," she said. "Ducks, hens, a pig, a horse!"

"I have the hat!" said Max.
"Beth is not the farmer!"

"I will take that hat, Max!"
Dave said.

"Stop it, Max and Dave!" said
Grace. "Let us make masks."

Old MacDonald
★ Hens = Beth and Grace
★ Pig = Dave
★ Duck = Max
★ Farmer = ?

On his page, Max made a duck
mask with tape. Beth made hens.

Dave made a pig mask on his page.

"That is an odd pig," Grace said.

"It takes ages to make this horse mask, Meg," said Jake.

"I can make this mask fast, Jake," said Meg.

Meg made a fat gerbil mask.

"Place that gerbil in a paper cage."
Jake gave a grin.

"Take your places up on stage," said Grace.

"Grunt!" Dave had on his pig mask.

"Squeak!" said Meg.

"Quack!" Max had on his duck mask.

"Cluck!" Beth had on her hen mask.

"Look at that cat!" said Grace.
"That is an odd farmer!"

Envision It! | Retell

Think Critically

1. If you were in Beth's class, which character in the play would you be? Text to Self

2. Why do you think the author waited until the end to show the cat? Think Like an Author

3. Why did the children forget about the farmer's hat?

   Cause and Effect

4. Look back on page 63. What clues could you use from the picture or the words to find out what a gerbil is? Monitor and Clarify

5. **Look Back and Write** Look back at pages 60–63. Write about an actor in the play. Use evidence in the selection to support your answer.

   TEST PRACTICE Extended Response

Pat Cummings

Pat Cummings once played a rabbit in a school play, and her sister played a grasshopper. Ms. Cummings made the cat the farmer in this story because "cats seem to naturally find the center of attention."

Ms. Cummings loves writing children's books. "The best part is that I can explore almost any subject."

Here are other books by Pat Cummings.

Use the Reading Log in the *Reader's and Writer's Notebook* to record your independent reading.

Read Together

Let's Write It!

Key Features of a Brief Composition

● tells interesting facts

● tells about one topic

READING STREET ONLINE
GRAMMAR JAMMER
www.ReadingStreet.com

Brief Composition

A **brief composition** tells information about real people or things. The student model on the next page is an example of a brief composition.

Writing Prompt Think about ways children work together at school. Now write about one thing children at your school do together.

Writer's Checklist

Remember, you should ...

☑ write about a real thing that children do together at your school.

☑ write in complete sentences.

☑ include at least one proper noun in your composition.

Every Friday we clean our classroom at Parker School.
We make our desks neat.
Eric wipes the board. Jo puts books away.
We keep our room clean.
We like to help.

Writing Trait Sentences

This composition is made up of complete **sentences.**

The name *Eric* is an example of a **proper noun**.

Genre Composition

This **brief composition** tells about real people.

Conventions

● **Proper Nouns**

Remember Special names for people, places, animals, and things are called **proper nouns**. Proper nouns begin with capital letters.

Max took the hat from **B**eth.

Social Studies in Reading

Genre
Expository Text

- Expository text is informational text that tells about real people, animals, places, or events.

- An expository text selection has a main idea. The main idea is the most important idea in the selection. Facts or details tell more about the main idea.

- An expository text selection usually has photographs that help explain the words.

- As you read "Helping Hands at 4-H," think about what you know about expository text. Then tell the main idea.

Read Together

Helping Hands at 4-H
by Lindy Russell

Where could you see what farmers do? At a 4-H club!

How old are kids in 4-H? They can be ages 8 to 18.

At 4-H you can take care of a horse or a pig.

Let's Think About...

What facts or details do you learn on these two pages? **Expository Text**

Let's **Think** About...

How does the photograph help you understand the words on this page?
Expository Text

You can get the eggs from the hens.

72

This 4-H club has a bake sale.
They place an ad in the paper.
They sell eggs too.

Let's Think About...

What details does the photograph tell that the words do not? **Expository Text**

Bake Sale

Eggs
$ 2.00

The sale is good!
The club will get chicks.

Let's **Think** About...

What is the main idea of this selection?
Expository Text

The chicks will get big.
Then the club will have lots
of eggs to sell.

Let's **Think** About...

What facts or details tell more about the main idea?
Expository Text

Let's **Think** About...

Reading Across Texts In *The Farmer in the Hat* and "Helping Hands at 4-H," groups of children work together. What is each group trying to do? Why?

Writing Across Texts The children in both groups work well together. Why is that important? Write your ideas.

Let's Learn It!

Read Together

READING STREET ONLINE
VOCABULARY ACTIVITIES
www.ReadingStreet.com

Classroom Rules
- We take turns.
- We raise our hand before we speak.
- We keep our desks clean.

Listening and Speaking

Get Ready For Grade 2

Answer a listener's questions.

Share Information and Ideas When we share information and ideas, we speak clearly. We tell others important details. We answer questions if listeners do not understand.

Practice It! Think of two classroom rules. Tell the rules to others. Speak clearly and slowly, using people's names and the conventions of language.

Vocabulary

When we want to describe when things happen, we use **time-order words.**

first

next

last

Practice It! Read these words. Write sentences using each word.

yesterday   **today**   **tomorrow**

Fluency

Appropriate Phrasing When you see an exclamation mark at the end of a sentence, use your voice to show a strong feeling.

Practice It!

1. Look! Pat made a paper mask!

2. I did not think the skit could be this fun!

3. Run! We could be late for the play!

Objectives
● Listen closely to speakers and ask questions to help you better understand the topic. ● Share information and ideas about the topic. Speak at the correct pace.

Oral Vocabulary

Let's Talk About

Read Together

People in Communities

● Share ideas about people in our community.

● Discuss who works to make our community a nice place.

● Share information about jobs people have in our community.

READING STREET ONLINE
CONCEPT TALK VIDEO
www.ReadingStreet.com

You've learned **1 1 0** Amazing Words so far this year!

Phonemic Awareness

Let's Listen for

Sounds

● Find three things that begin with the sound /ch/. Say each sound in the words.

● Find something that rhymes with *sit*. Now change the short *i* sound to a long *i* sound. Say the new word.

● Find something that begins with the same sound you hear at the beginning of the word *whip*.

● Find something that rhymes with *stone*. Say each sound in the word.

● Find two things that rhyme with *side*.

READING STREET ONLINE
SOUND-SPELLING CARDS
www.ReadingStreet.com

Read Together

Long *i: i_e*

Words I Can Blend

h	i	d	e

| p | i | l | e |

| s | l | i | m | e |

| p | r | i | d | e |

| k | i | t | e |

Sentences I Can Read

1. That big bug came to hide in this pile of black slime.

2. Kip takes pride in his kite.

Words I Can Read

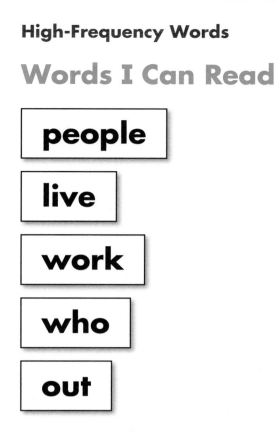

people

live

work

who

out

Sentences I Can Read

1. People who live in this place ride bikes to work.

2. Five mice ran out to hide on that vine.

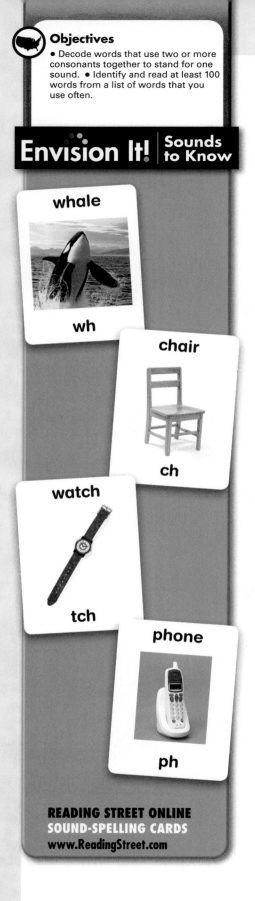

Envision It! | Sounds to Know

whale
wh

chair
ch

watch
tch

phone
ph

READING STREET ONLINE
SOUND-SPELLING CARDS
www.ReadingStreet.com

Phonics

Digraphs *wh, ch, tch, ph*

Words I Can Blend

ch e ck

wh i ch

g r a ph

wh i t e

d i tch

Sentences I Can Read

1. Check which graph can help.

2. Did that white hat drop in the ditch?

I Can Read!

People who live on this lane like to work out. Mike and Chuck ride bikes. Phil and Jane run on the path.

Mom and Dad catch fish in Duck Lake. Beth swims. Jill hikes on the hill. Which is best?

You've learned

- Long *i: i_e*
- Consonant Digraphs *wh, ch, tch, ph*

High-Frequency Words
people live work
who out

Who Works Here?

by Melissa Blackwell Burke

illustrated by Tim Spransy

 **Genre**

Expository text tells about real people and events. Next you will read about real people who live and work in a neighborhood. What do you want to find out? Set a purpose for reading.

Question of the Week

Who works to make our community a nice place?

People live and work
in this neighborhood.
It is such a busy place.

Who works in this place?
Phil will talk to them.
They all like to help us.

I help us all stay safe.
When you ride your bike, stop
and check all ways.
I will help you cross.

I help stop fires. Fire can be bad.
All of us must be safe from fire.

I drop mail in this box. This man will stop and wave and smile. This man likes to chat a while.

I drive this big bus.
People can ride this big bus. This
bus will stop and pick them up.

I pick up trash.
When it is set out,
I will pitch it in this big truck.

Who works where you live?
Smile at them like Phil.
You will like them!

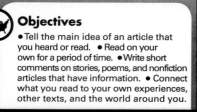

Envision It! | Retell

Think Critically

1. This selection is about workers in a community. What other community job might someone have?

Text to World

2. Why do you think the author used photographs in this selection? Think Like an Author

3. What do you think the author wants you to know?

Author's Purpose

4. What did you learn about workers in a community by reading this selection?

Important Ideas

5. Look Back and Write Look back at pages 90 and 91. Write about the job of one of the people you see.

TEST PRACTICE | Extended Response

Melissa Blackwell Burke

Melissa Blackwell Burke grew up in a small town in Texas. She loved to visit the library. She says, "When I was a little girl, I wanted to be many things, including a teacher, a newspaper reporter, and a librarian. I have been two of those—a teacher and a newspaper reporter. Who knows—I might still become a librarian some day!"

Here are other books about neighborhood workers.

Use the Reading Log in the *Reader's and Writer's Notebook* to record your independent reading.

Expository

Let's Write It!

Read Together

Key Features of an Explanation

● tells about a person, idea, or thing

● helps people understand the topic

**READING STREET ONLINE
GRAMMAR JAMMER**
www.ReadingStreet.com

Explanation

An **explanation** tells about real people, ideas, or things. It helps a reader understand the topic. The student model on the next page is an example of an explanation.

Writing Prompt Think about the jobs people do. Now think about a job you think is interesting. Write a brief explanation of the job.

Writer's Checklist

Remember, you should ...

☑ tell about what a real person does at work.

☑ use capital letters and punctuation correctly.

☑ capitalize titles, such as Mr., Mrs., Ms., or Dr.

A Teacher's Job

Mrs. Taylor is a teacher.

She teaches children to read.

She teaches them how to do

math and spelling.

Mrs. Taylor loves children.

Writing Trait Conventions

Use capital letters for names when you write. Use periods at the end of sentences.

The **special title** Mrs. begins with a capital letter and ends with a period.

Genre Explanation

The author thinks a teacher's job is interesting. The author explains what a teacher does.

Conventions

Special Titles

A **title** can come before the name of a person. A title begins with a capital letter. Some titles end with a period.

Officer Black   **Ms.** Timms   **Dr.** Pak

Genre
Procedural Text

Read Together

● Maps use words along with map features, including signs and symbols.

● Signs and symbols on a map help you know where you are and which way you can go.

● A compass rose is a symbol that shows you the directions north, east, south, and west. These directions are usually abbreviated N, E, S, and W.

● As you read "Neighborhood Map," think about what you've learned about signs and symbols in procedural text.

Neighborhood Map

 This shows people where to wait for a bus.

 This tells drivers to stop.

 This tells drivers to let other drivers go first.

 This means drivers may only drive in one direction on the street.

 This means that a train may cross.

 This means pedestrians may cross.

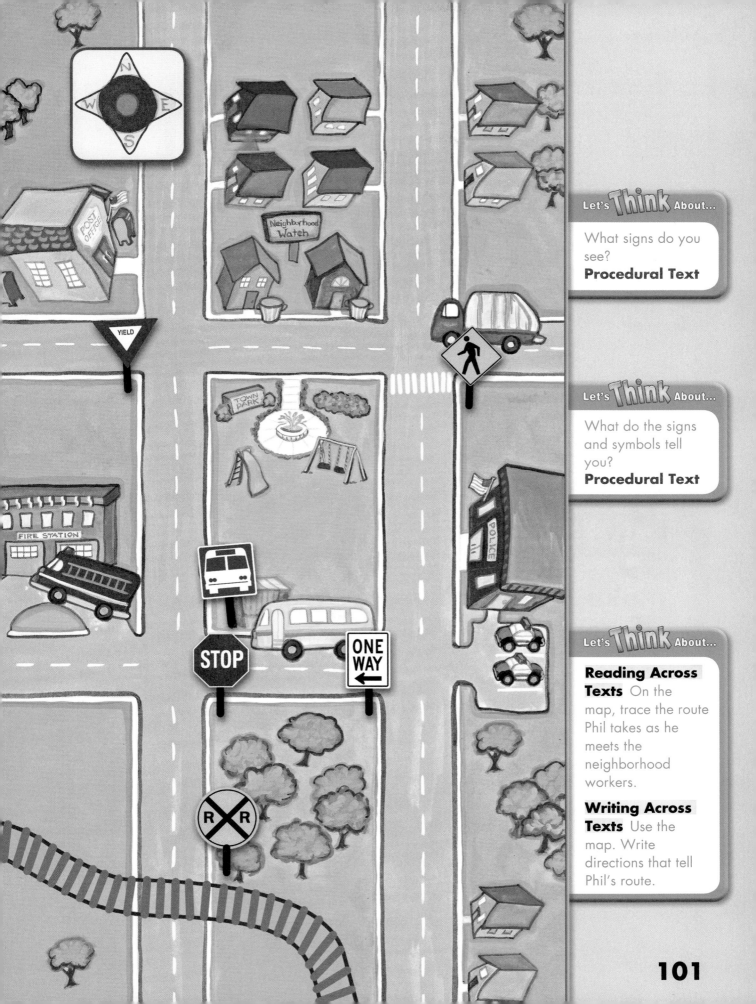

Let's **Think** About...

What signs do you see?
Procedural Text

Let's **Think** About...

What do the signs and symbols tell you?
Procedural Text

Let's **Think** About...

Reading Across Texts On the map, trace the route Phil takes as he meets the neighborhood workers.

Writing Across Texts Use the map. Write directions that tell Phil's route.

101

Don't forget about our trip to the science museum on Friday! We will leave at 9:00 in the morning. Ms. Chase will collect money for ...

Let's Learn It!

Read Together

READING STREET ONLINE
VOCABULARY ACTIVITIES
www.ReadingStreet.com

Get Ready For Grade 2

Make eye contact with listeners.

Listening and Speaking

Make Announcements When we make an announcement, we remember to speak loudly enough to be heard. We make eye contact with listeners. We tell all of the information.

Practice It! Make an announcement to the class about a field trip. Tell when you are going, where you are going, and what time you will leave. Use proper nouns, such as names of teachers.

Vocabulary

Direction words tell us where things are and how to get from place to place.

above

below

Above and *below* are direction words.

Practice It! Write instructions on how to get from your classroom to the library. Use direction words.

Fluency

Appropriate Phrasing When you come to a period, you know it is the end of a sentence. Stop when you reach the period to show when the sentence ends.

Practice It!

1. I live with Mom, Dad, and Jack.

2. My cat likes to go out and catch mice.

Oral Vocabulary

Let's Talk About

Read Together

Communities in Nature

● Share information about communities in nature.

● Share information about animals and animal behavior.

● Contribute to a discussion about how animal communities work together to survive.

READING STREET ONLINE
CONCEPT TALK VIDEO
www.ReadingStreet.com

Let's Listen for

Sounds

● Find something that rhymes with *nod*. Change the short *o* sound to a long *o* sound. Say the new word.

● Find five things that contain the long *o* sound.

● Find two things that rhyme with *cone*. Say the sounds in each word.

READING STREET ONLINE
SOUND-SPELLING CARDS
www.ReadingStreet.com

Read Together

106

Envision It! | **Sounds to Know**

rope

o_e

Phonics

🎯 Long *o: o_e*

Words I Can Blend

| s | t | o | n | e |

| b | r | o | k | e |

| h | o | p | e |

| m | o | l | e |

| h | o | l | e |

Sentences I Can Read

1. That stone broke the glass.

2. I hope that mole can spot its hole.

Words I Can Read

there

down

inside

now

together

Sentences I Can Read

1. Take down that note and place it there inside his desk.

2. Now those kids can all walk together.

Objectives
- Identify and read contractions.
- Identify and read at least 100 words from a list of words that you use often.

Envision It! | Sounds to Know

can + not = can't

contraction

she + will = she'll

contraction

I + am = I'm

contraction

Phonics

Contractions

Words I Can Blend

Sentences I Can Read

1. It is odd that Lin can't tell if it'll be nice out, isn't it?

2. I'm glad Pam didn't get lost.

I Can Read!

Josh and Grace spoke on the phone together. Josh is sick, and he'll rest inside for now.

Grace said, "That's too bad. There is class work that you'll want. Let's get together. I'm close and can get it down to you."

You've learned

◉ Long o: o_e
◉ Contractions

High-Frequency Words
there   down   inside
now   together

The Big Circle

by Eric Kimmel

illustrated by Richard Bernal

Genre

Stories that are **fiction** are made-up stories. Next you will read a made-up story about dinosaurs.

Read Together

How do animal communities work together to survive?

Big T. Rex wakes up.
Big T. Rex wants his lunch,
but not bones and not stones.

Big T. Rex wants meat.

This is a herd of triceratops.
This herd is walking home.

At home this herd can get
grass. Munching grass
at home will make them fat.

Sniff, sniff. Big T. Rex smells with his nose. "Hmm," said Big T. Rex.

"This nose smells a baby. I can hunt it. I'll get it and it will make a good lunch. Yum, yum!"

Big T. Rex rose up on his back legs.
Big T. Rex ran up the slope and down.
The herd saw Big T. Rex run.

It was time to make a big circle. The small animals went inside the circle. The baby went inside too.

Big T. Rex didn't like this.
Big T. Rex couldn't get his lunch.

But Big T. Rex didn't quit. "I'll make them run."

But the herd didn't run.
They kept still and close together
in the big circle.

Then they gave Big T. Rex a poke and a bump. They drove him back.

Big T. Rex ran back up the slope. Those triceratops saw Big T. Rex run. Now all are safe.

They will walk home and then munch grass there. Big T. Rex can't get them. The herd is safe.

Envision It! Retell

READING STREET ONLINE
STORY SORT
www.ReadingStreet.com

Think Critically

1. How do other kinds of animals protect their babies? Text to World

2. What does the author want you to learn in this story? Author's Purpose

3. What happened after Big T. Rex saw the baby triceratops? Sequence

4. Why did the herd of triceratops make a big circle? Inferring

5. Look Back and Write Look back at page 125. Write about how this animal community helped each other. Give evidence from the story to support your answer. Discuss what you wrote with a partner.

TEST PRACTICE Extended Response

Eric Kimmel

As a boy, Eric Kimmel visited the Museum of Natural History in New York City almost every weekend. "The dinosaur skeletons were old friends," he says. "Triceratops and stegosaurus were my favorites."

Richard Bernal

Richard Bernal drew the pictures for this story. "I love dinosaurs," he says. "I have several dinosaur toys in my studio."

Here are other books by Eric Kimmel and Richard Bernal.

Use the Reading Log in the *Reader's and Writer's Notebook* to record your independent reading.

Let's Write It!

Read Together

Key Features of a Poem

● it can describe an event

● the lines may rhyme

READING STREET ONLINE
GRAMMAR JAMMER
www.ReadingStreet.com

Poem

A **poem** is a short piece of writing. The writer uses lines of well-chosen words. Some words in poems may rhyme.

Writing Prompt Think about how animals protect themselves. Now write a poem about an animal that protects itself from an enemy.

Writer's Checklist

Remember, you should . . .

☑ tell how the animal protects itself.

☑ describe an event in an order that makes sense.

☑ make sure you begin proper nouns with a capital letter.

☑ say your poem aloud.

It is Friday.

Fox wants lunch.

She needs to catch!

She likes to munch!

Hurry, Turtle! Time to hide!

Turtle must hide inside.

Turtle hides inside his shell.

Turtle can hide so well!

This **proper noun** begins with a capital letter.

Writing Trait Organization
The lines of the poem show what happens in sequence.

Genre
This **poem** has lines that rhyme to sound more interesting. Say the poem aloud.

Conventions

- **Days, Months, and Holidays**

  Remember Days of the week, **months**, and **holidays** all begin with capital letters.

  Mother's Day is a **Sunday** in **May.**

Genre
Literary Nonfiction

● Literary nonfiction tells about real people, animals, places, or events.

● Literary nonfiction has a main idea and facts or details that tell more about the main idea.

● Literary nonfiction usually has some elements of a story, such as characters, plot, or setting.

● Read "We Are Safe Together." What did you learn about literary nonfiction that helps you better understand this selection?

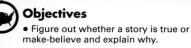

We Are Safe Together

by Julia Nasser

illustrated by Chris Boyd

a school of fish

I'm a fish. A lake is my home. I swim with many fish. I'm inside this big circle. We stick together to be safe.

a herd of zebra

I'm a baby zebra. Grassland is my home. There are big zebras in this herd. We can run fast. We stick together to be safe.

Let's Think About...

What clues on these pages tell you this is literary nonfiction?
Literary Nonfiction

a flock of birds

Let's Think About...

Is this selection true or a fantasy? How do you know?
Literary Nonfiction

I'm a bird. I bend down to dig up my lunch. I'm with my flock. We can go up fast. We stick together to be safe.

a herd of triceratops

I'm a triceratops. I don't live
here now. I ate grass and plants.
I walked with a big herd.
We stuck together to be safe.

Let's **Think** About...

What is the main idea of this selection? **Literary Nonfiction**

Let's **Think** About...

Reading Across Texts How is what happens in *The Big Circle* similar to what happens in "We Are Safe Together"?

Writing Across Texts Write the facts you learned about triceratops in *The Big Circle* and "We Are Safe Together."

135

Objectives
● Read fluently and understand texts at your grade level. ● Identify and put words into groups based on what they mean. ● Listen closely to speakers and ask questions to help you better understand the topic.

Let's Learn It!

Read Together

READING STREET ONLINE
VOCABULARY ACTIVITIES
www.ReadingStreet.com

Listening and Speaking

Get Ready For Grade 2

Use good listening and speaking skills, even in conversations with friends.

Informal Conversations When we have conversations with friends, we pay attention to the speaker. We speak clearly when it is our turn to speak.

Practice It! Have a conversation with others about how animal communities work together to survive. Follow the rules. Speak clearly and slowly, using the conventions of language. Be a good listener and a good speaker.

Vocabulary

When we **sort words,** we put them into groups that make sense.

tiger

zebra

A *tiger* eats meat. A *zebra* eats plants.

Practice It! Read the names of these animals. Identify and sort them into groups of plant eaters and meat eaters.

lion   horse   deer   rabbit

Fluency

Accuracy and Rate Read the sentences. When you read, read the words you see. Blend the sounds to read the word. Check by putting the new word in the sentence to see if it makes sense.

Practice It!

1. We'll write a note to Steph together.

2. I can't ride my bike down the hill.

3. Isn't it good to be inside the school?

Oral Vocabulary

Let's Talk About

Read Together

Communities in Nature

- Share information about communities in nature.

- Share information about animals and plants.

- Share ideas about how plant and animal communities are important to each other.

READING STREET ONLINE
CONCEPT TALK VIDEO
www.ReadingStreet.com

Objectives

- Tell the difference between long- and short-vowel sounds in words that have one syllable.
- Combine sounds together to say words with one and two syllables.
- Break up one-syllable words into each sound that makes up the word.

Let's Listen for

Sounds

Read Together

- Find four things that contain the long *u* sound. Say each sound in one of the words.

- Find something that rhymes with *rub*. Change the short *u* sound to a long *u* sound. Say the new word.

- Find something that contains the long *e* sound.

READING STREET ONLINE
SOUND-SPELLING CARDS
www.ReadingStreet.com

Envision It! | **Sounds to Know**

mule

u_e

concrete

e_e

READING STREET ONLINE
SOUND-SPELLING CARDS
www.ReadingStreet.com

Phonics

Long *u: u_e;* Long *e: e_e*

Words I Can Blend

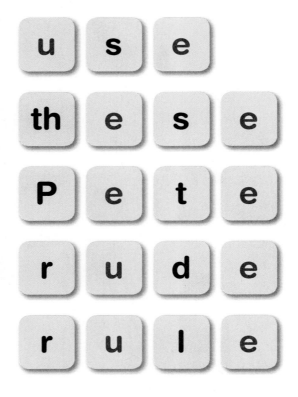

u s e

th e s e

P e t e

r u d e

r u l e

Sentences I Can Read

1. Jack can use these white socks.

2. Pete made a rule that kids can't act rude.

Words I Can Read

grow

food

around

find

water

under

Sentences I Can Read

1. Will food grow on this land around his home?

2. Steve can find cute fish under the water.

Envision It! | Sounds to Know

filled

ending -ed

jumped

ending -ed

twisted

ending -ed

READING STREET ONLINE
SOUND-SPELLING CARDS
www.ReadingStreet.com

Phonics

Inflected Ending *-ed*

Words I Can Blend

c a l l e d

t a l k e d

m u n ch e d

a d d e d

p r i n t e d

Sentences I Can Read

1. Vic called Lill and talked as he munched on lunch.

2. Jon printed his name and added six and nine.

I Can Read!

Food can grow in odd places. June and Gene watched as fish munched on plants under water.

Pete helped us find snacks that bugs like around rocks. Dad planted yams in this big tub.

Plants can get big in many places. If these plants make food, let's find good places that they can grow.

You've learned

- Long *u*: *u_e*; Long *e*: *e_e*
- Inflected Ending *-ed*

High-Frequency Words
grow   food   around
find   water   under

Life in the Forest

by Claire Daniel

Genre

Expository text tells facts about real places. Next you will read about the plants and animals in a forest.

How are plant and animal communities important to each other?

We can find life in the forest.
It is a busy place!

Sun helped these leaves get wide and flat.

Sun shines on the leaves and helps them grow. Bugs like munching on them. Yum, yum! Bugs can eat lots and lots.

This woodpecker sits on a branch.
Peck! Peck! Peck!
It pecks to get at bugs.

These holes tell us
that woodpeckers
pecked on this tree.

This huge log is soft and damp.
Water has made this log rot.
Small bugs made homes in this log.

This bird hops on this log
and then pecks at it. Yum, yum!
It gets bugs when it pecks.

Nuts grow on trees and then fall all around. Squirrels get nuts and munch on them. Yum, yum!

A fox is cute, but it likes to catch small animals.

This black bear eats grass, nuts, and grubs. Grubs are small bugs that hide under rocks and logs.

This bear picked up these rocks and hunted for grubs.

This hummingbird uses its bill to get food. It sticks its bill in this plant.

Many plants have shapes like tubes. Small hummingbirds can sip from these plants.

Hummingbirds can catch
small bugs too.

This big forest is filled with life.
Many animals and plants call it home.
It is a busy place!

Envision It! Retell

READING STREET ONLINE
STORY SORT
www.ReadingStreet.com

Think Critically

1. How are the dinosaurs in *The Big Circle* different from the animals mentioned in *Life in the Forest?* Text to Text

2. Why does the author use captions with some photographs? Think Like an Author

3. Why do you think the author wrote *Life in the Forest?* Author's Purpose

4. What did you already know about trees that helped you understand this selection?

   Background Knowledge

5. **Look Back and Write** Look back at pages 158 and 159. Write about one animal that lives in the forest. Use evidence from the selection to support your answer.

   TEST PRACTICE Extended Response

Meet the Author

Claire Daniel

Claire Daniel learned about forests on a three-month hiking trip with her husband. "That was an amazing experience—being in the forest and living in it."

A bear came to their campsite once. "We heard him coming, so we ran to a shelter. It was a frightening experience! The bear went into our tent and then backed out of it, not finding any food."

Here are more books by Claire Daniel.

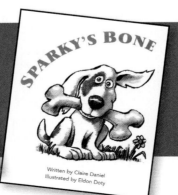

 Use the Reading Log in the *Reader's and Writer's Notebook* to record your independent reading.

Objectives
- Write short nonfiction essays about topics you like.
- Understand and use nouns when reading, writing, and speaking.

Let's Write It!

Read Together

Key Features of a Description

- tells about real people or things
- uses descriptive words
- can tell how things look

READING STREET ONLINE
GRAMMAR JAMMER
www.ReadingStreet.com

Description

A **description** tells about real things. It can tell how things look or sound. The student model on the next page is an example of a description.

Writing Prompt Think about how plants and animals are important to each other. Now write a description about how an animal uses plants to survive.

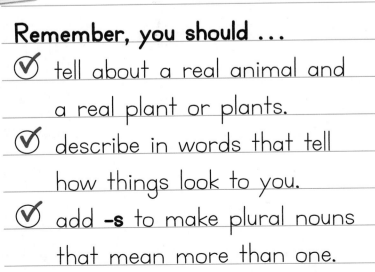

Writer's Checklist

Remember, you should . . .

☑ tell about a real animal and a real plant or plants.

☑ describe in words that tell how things look to you.

☑ add **-s** to make plural nouns that mean more than one.

Squirrels Need Trees

Squirrels live in trees.

Squirrels eat the nuts that grow on trees.

I think squirrels look cute when they look for nuts.

These **nouns** that end in **-s** tell about more than one squirrel or tree or nut.

Writing Trait Voice
This writer shows voice by saying squirrels are cute.

Genre Description
This description tells about real squirrels.

Conventions

● **Singular and Plural Nouns**

Remember Many nouns add **-s** to mean more than one. Say the plural nouns.

nut + s = nuts bug + s = bugs

Science in Reading

Genre
Magazine Article

● A magazine article is expository text that tells about a topic.

● The article has facts about the topic.

● The article may have pictures. They help us understand the topic.

● The article may also have a Table of Contents. The Table of Contents, including titles and page numbers, can help us locate specific information in the article.

● Read "A Mangrove Forest." As you read, look for elements of a magazine article.

A Mangrove Forest

by Terry Lynk
illustrated by Russell Farrell

Read Together

Table of Contents

Animals

Lots of animals live here.

Some live in the water.

Some live out of the water.

They are all around this forest.

Fish

Have you watched fish swim under a tree?

You can find fish in this forest.

These trees grow in salt water.

Fish swim under the trees.

Let's Think About...

Find the Table of Contents. How can you use it to find information in this article? **Magazine Article**

Let's Think About...

How can you use the title "Fish" in the Table of Contents to find information? **Magazine Article**

Let's Think About...

What clues can you use from the picture or the words to find out who lives in the forest? **Magazine Article**

Food

Fish find food in the water. Birds can use fish and bugs as food.

Save the Forests

Some forests like this are being lost. We must save these forests.

Let's **Think** About...

How does this photograph help you understand the article?
Magazine Article

Let's **Think** About...

What **important details** can you identify in the article?
Magazine Article

Let's **Think** About...

Reading Across Texts How are the forests in *Life in the Forest* and "A Mangrove Forest" alike? How are they different?

Writing Across Texts Write sentences about each forest.

READING STREET ONLINE
VOCABULARY ACTIVITIES
www.ReadingStreet.com

Get Ready For Grade 2

Use the conventions of language when sharing information.

Listening and Speaking

Share Information and Ideas When we share information and ideas with others, we speak clearly. When others share information and ideas with us, we listen carefully.

Practice It! Ask others how plant and animal communities help each other. Share your ideas. Speak clearly and slowly. Use plural nouns for things. Listen carefully.

Vocabulary

If a word has more than one meaning, you can use nearby words, or **context clues,** to understand which meaning is being used. The word *place* can mean "the space where someone or something is." *Place* can also mean "to put something somewhere."

Practice It! Read these sentences. What is the meaning of the word *place* in each sentence?

The forest is an amazing **place.**
The bird will **place** a twig on the nest.

Fluency

Appropriate Phrasing When you come to a period, you know it is the end of a sentence. Stop when you reach the period to show when the sentence ends.

Practice It!

1. Pete saw a bear eat his food.

2. The cute pup wanted to sip water.

● Listen closely to speakers and ask questions to help you better understand the topic. ● Share information and ideas about the topic. Speak at the correct pace.

Let's Talk About

Communities in Nature

● Recall how people work together in a community.

● Share information about insects and insect behavior.

● Take part in a discussion about how an insect community is like a community of people.

READING STREET ONLINE
CONCEPT TALK VIDEO
www.ReadingStreet.com

You've learned
1 3 4
Amazing Words
so far this year!

Objectives
- Tell the difference between long- and short-vowel sounds in words that have one syllable.
- Combine sounds together to say words with one and two syllables.

Let's Listen for

Sounds

Read Together

- Find something that rhymes with *bed*. Change the short *e* sound to a long *e* sound. Say the new word.

- Find four things that contain the long *e* sound.

- Find three things that contain the short *a* sound and have two syllables.

- Find something that rhymes with *mitten*. Say each sound in the word.

**READING STREET ONLINE
SOUND-SPELLING CARDS
www.ReadingStreet.com**

173

Objectives
● Decode words by using letter-sound patterns to understand the different sounds vowels make. ● Decode words that use two vowels to make one sound. ● Identify and read at least 100 words from a list of words that you use often.

Envision It! | Sounds to Know

we

-e

bee

ee

READING STREET ONLINE
SOUND-SPELLING CARDS
www.ReadingStreet.com

Phonics

Long *e: e, ee*

Words I Can Blend

sh	e
s	ee
f	ee	l
w	e
n	ee	d

Sentences I Can Read

1. Can't she see that we need that desk?

2. Pat ate too much and didn't feel well.

Words I Can Read

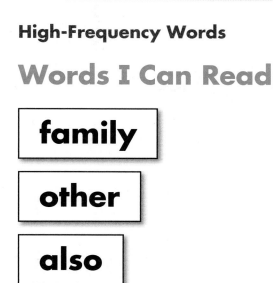

Sentences I Can Read

1. That bee family also can see the other side of that hive.

2. Their new home has some big trees.

Phonics

Syllables VC/CV

Words I Can Blend

r a b b i t

b a s k e t

m i s t a k e

t a d p o l e

i n s i d e

Sentences I Can Read

1. We set his pet rabbit in its basket.

2. Will it be a mistake to keep that tadpole inside?

Lee and Sam like to invent new stuff. When they see a need, these kids fix it. Their family admits some of the stuff is odd.

Lee made mittens for his pet reptile. He also invented zigzag buttons. Sam came up with a picnic basket for his kitten. Will Lee and Sam make other stuff? We will see!

You've learned

- Long e: e, ee
- Syllables VC/CV

High-Frequency Words
family   other   also
their   some   new

177

Honey Bees

by Jesús Cervantes

illustrated by Tom Leonard

Genre

Expository text tells facts about real people, places, animals, or things. This article tells about honey bees.

Question of the Week

How is an insect community like a community of people?

The sun shines. These honey bees wake
up. It is time for these insects to work.

Buzz,
    buzz,
        buzz.

In the hive, bees live like a family.
In the hive we can see there is a
queen bee, lots of worker bees,
and some drones.

This is the queen bee.
She rules the hive.

These bees are drones.
Drones help the queen bee.

This hive is hidden in a big tree.
Worker bees will keep this hive safe.

It is not wise to make bees mad! Mad
bees will attack.

Worker bees make wax cells in the hive. These wax cells are small holes.

Bees save honey in some wax cells. Small bees live and grow big in other cells.

Bees feed on honey. Worker bees feed honey to other bees in the hive. Bees make honey from nectar.

Bees get nectar inside flowers.
Bees take this sweet nectar back home.

Bees also get pollen from flowers.

Worker bees feed pollen to
the queen bee and small bees.
It helps them get big.

When those small bees get big,
it is time to make a new hive.

Worker bees make the new hive.
A new queen bee will go with them.

When it gets cold, these bees will go inside their hive and sleep and rest. The bees will wake up when the sun shines.

Envision It! Retell

READING STREET ONLINE
STORY SORT
www.ReadingStreet.com

Think Critically

1. Worker bees have important jobs. What important jobs do you have at home or school? Text to Self

2. What does the author want you to learn about in *Honey Bees?* Author's Purpose

3. How are queen bees and worker bees alike and different? Compare and Contrast

4. Look back at pages 186–187. What questions would you ask to find out about how people get honey to eat? Questioning

5. Look Back and Write Look back at page 183. What is the queen bee's job? Use evidence from the selection to support your answer.

TEST PRACTICE Extended Response

Meet the Author

Jesús Cervantes

Jesús Cervantes grew up on a lemon and avocado ranch in southern California. He says, "The ranch had lots of bees. They were brought in to pollinate the trees. I wasn't afraid of bees when I was growing up."

Mr. Cervantes thinks bees are great. He says, "I love honey when it's still on the comb."

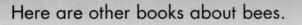

Here are other books about bees.

THE HONEY MAKERS
GAIL GIBBONS

EYEWITNESS READERS
Busy buzzy bee

Use the Reading Log in the *Reader's and Writer's Notebook* to record your independent reading.

Objectives
● Write short nonfiction essays about topics you like. ● Understand and use nouns when reading, writing, and speaking.

Let's Write It!

Read Together

Key Features of an Expository Paragraph

● tells about and explains real things

● can describe the things

READING STREET ONLINE
GRAMMAR JAMMER
www.ReadingStreet.com

Expository Paragraph

An **expository paragraph** explains real things. The student model on the next page is an example of an expository paragraph.

Writing Prompt Think about another kind of insect that lives in a community. Now write a paragraph about that insect community.

Writer's Checklist

Remember, you should . . .

☑ explain or describe a real insect community.

☑ write sentences about the topic.

☑ make sure each sentence in your paragraph has at least one noun.

Ants

Ants live together. Little ants have big jobs. Some ants find food. Some ants take care of the queen.

This **noun, ants,** names a kind of insect. The sentence is about ants.

Writing Trait Focus
Each sentence is about the main topic.

Genre Expository Paragraph
This writer explains how ants live together.

Conventions

● **Nouns in Sentences**

Remember Nouns name persons, places, animals, or things. A noun can be in more than one place in a sentence.

The **hives** are hidden in a **tree.**

Genre
Poetry

- A poem is written in lines. Lines of poetry form groups of lines. These groups of lines are called stanzas.

- A poem often rhymes. This means words at the ends of some lines have the same middle and ending sounds.

- A poem often has rhythm. This means it has a regular pattern of beats that you can hear.

- As you read "Under a Rock" and "Night Song," think about rhyme and rhythm.

Read Together

Under a Rock

Lift up a rock
and you will see
a busy bug
community.

by Betsy Franco
illustrated by Chris Lensch

Night Song

When the sun has set
And night has come,
The insect chorus
Starts to hum.

And nothing else
Is there to hear,
But the insect voices
Soft and clear.

The insects hum
In sweet delight,
Singing their praises
Of the night.

by Leland B. Jacobs
illustrated by Chris Lensch

Let's Think About...

What are the **rhyming words** in each poem? Does each poem have **rhythm?** How can you tell?

Let's Think About...

How many lines are there in "Under a Rock"? How many stanzas are there in "Night Song"?

Let's Think About...

Reading Across Texts How are the bees in *Honey Bees* and the insects in these poems alike?

Writing Across Texts Write a short poem about insects. Use rhyming words and rhythm. Read your poem aloud.

Let's Learn It!

Read Together

READING STREET ONLINE
VOCABULARY ACTIVITIES
www.ReadingStreet.com

First, stand up straight. Second, reach high into the sky. Third, bend over and touch your toes. Fourth, stand back up!

Listening and Speaking

Get Ready For Grade 2

Listen carefully when someone is giving directions.

Follow Directions It is important to listen carefully to directions so that we can follow them correctly. Good listeners remember all the steps and can say them back.

Practice It! Listen to your teacher give directions on how to do jumping jacks. Listen carefully and say the steps back. Then follow the directions.

Vocabulary

An **antonym** is a word that means the opposite of another word.

full

empty

Full is an antonym of *empty.*

Practice It! Read the words. Write and say antonyms for each one.

hot   sad   up   day

Fluency

Accuracy and Rate Read the sentences. When you read, say the word you see. Blend the sounds to read the word. Put the word in the sentence. Ask yourself if it makes sense.

Practice It!

1. Britt's family will go on a picnic.

2. Did you see some cute kittens?

3. Steve has a hat with three buttons.

My School

chalkboard

map

chalk

teacher

books

computer

eraser

ruler

pencils

scissors

clock

bulletin board

school

playground

flag

student

crayon

cafeteria

table

classroom

chair

lunchbox

203

Where People Live

pueblo

cottage

apartment building

mobile home

204

houseboat

log cabin

high-rise

house

town house

Where Animals Live

den

barn

log

tree hollow

burrow

anthill

nest

hive

cave

doghouse

ocean

lodge

Where People Work

restaurant

construction site

farm

bank

store

office

hospital

How People Play

pretend

karate

inline skating

soccer

swimming

music

basketball

football

dance

art

My Town

school

grocery store

bus driver

post office

crossing guard

mail carrier

garbage collector

barbershop

library

librarian

barber

cashier

bus stop

fire truck

firefighter

police officer

park

gardener

213

Max and Ruby: A Big Fish for Max

catch
good
no
put
said
want

Who Works Here?

live
out
people
who
work

The Farmer in the Hat

be
could
horse
of
old
paper

The Big Circle

down
inside
now
there
together

Honey Bees

also
family
new
other
some
their

Life in the Forest

around
find
food
grow
under
water

Aa Bb Cc

Dd Ee Ff

Gg Hh Ii

Jj Kk Ll

Mm Nn Oo

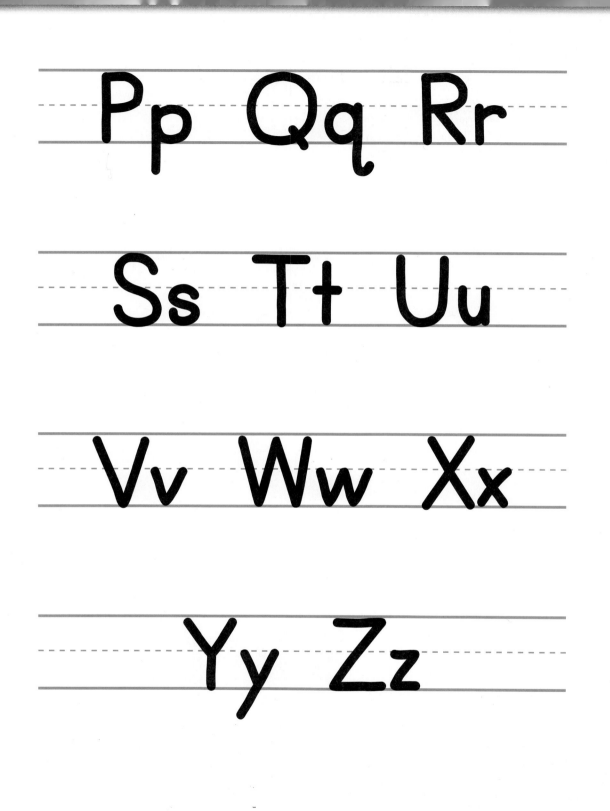

Pp Qq Rr

Ss Tt Uu

Vv Ww Xx

Yy Zz

Acknowledgments

Text

Grateful acknowledgment is made to the following for copyrighted material:

Page 198: "Under a Rock" from *Thematic Poetry: Creepy Crawlies* by Betsy Franco. Scholastic Inc./Teaching Resources. Copyright © 2000 by Betsy Franco. Reprinted by permission.

Page 199: "Night Song" from *Just Around the Corner* by Leland B. Jacobs. © 1993 by Allan D. Jacobs. Reprinted by permission of Henry Holt and Company, LLC.

Note: Every effort has been made to locate the copyright owner of material reproduced on this component. Omissions brought to our attention will be corrected in subsequent editions.

Illustrations

Cover Daniel Moreton
14 Ethan Long
19 Kathi Ember
20-33 Jody Wheeler
46 O'Kif
52-64 Pat Cummings
80 Bill McGuire
90-99 Tim Spransy
101 April Mosakowski Hartmann
108 Susan Mitchell
112-126 Richard Bernal
132-135 Chris Boyd
144 Doug Holgate
164-167 Russell Farrell
178 Kellie Lewis
178-193 Tom Leonard

Photographs

Every effort has been made to secure permission and provide appropriate credit for photographic material. The publisher deeply regrets any omission and pledges to correct errors called to its attention in subsequent editions.

Unless otherwise acknowledged, all photographs are the property of Pearson Education, Inc.

Photo locators denoted as follows: Top (T), Center (C), Bottom (B), Left (L), Right (R), Background (Bkgd)

10 (B) ©Tom Stewart/Corbis
12 (B) Masterfile Corporation
16 Jupiter Images
42 Alistair Berg/Photonica/Getty Images
44 (B) ©LWA-Dann Tardif/Corbis
71 Wagner Farm, Glenview Park District, Glenview, IL.
72 (B) Wagner Farm, Glenview Park District, Glenview, IL.
74 (CR, CL) G K & Vikki Hart/Getty Images
75 (B) Melanie Acevedo/FoodPix/Jupiter Images
78 ©Jeremy Woodhouse/Getty Images
137 Digital Vision, Mark Downey/Getty Images, Tom Bean/Corbis
138 ©John Cornell/Getty Images
146 (Bkgd) Bill Ross/Corbis
147 (CL) ©Royalty-Free/Corbis, (TR) Photowood Inc./Corbis, (TL) Steve Kaufman/Corbis
148 (BL) Tom Uhlman/Visuals Unlimited
151 (TR) Fritz Polking/Visuals Unlimited
152 (T) Jamie Harron; Papilio/Corbis
154 (T) Stephen Dalton/Photo Researchers, Inc.
155 (TR) Gerard Fuehrer/Visuals Unlimited, (B) Getty Images
156 (T) Jim Clare/Nature Picture Library
157 (T) Frederick D. Atwood
158 (CL) ©Gary W. Carter/Corbis, (BR) ©Royalty-Free/Corbis, (TL) Bill Dyer/Photo Researchers, Inc., (TR) Melissa Farlow/Aurora & Quanta Productions
159 (TL) Stephen Krasemann/Getty Images, (BR) Tim Thompson/Corbis
167 (C) Theo Allofs/Danita Delimont, Agent
168 Vernon Leach/Alamy
170 ©Premaphotos/Nature Picture Library
201 (TL) ©Jonelle Weave/Getty Images, (TR) Jupiter Image.

Identify and read the high-frequency words that you have learned this year. How many words can you read?

Unit R.1
a
green
I
see

Unit R.2
like
one
we

Unit R.3
do
look
was
yellow
you

Unit R.4
are
have
that
they
two

Unit R.5
he
is
three
to
with

Unit R.6
for
go
here
me
where

Unit 1.1
come
my
way

Unit 1.2
she
take
up
what

Unit 1.3
blue
from
help
little
use

Unit 1.4
eat
five
four
her

this
too

Unit 1.5
saw
small
tree
your

Unit 1.6
home
into
many
them

Unit 2.1
catch
good
no
put
said
want

Unit 2.2
be
could
horse
of
old
paper

Unit 2.3
live
out
people
who
work

Unit 2.4
down
inside
now
there
together

Unit 2.5
around
find
food
grow
under
water

Unit 2.6
also
family
new
other
some
their

219

High-Frequency Words

Unit 3.1
always
become
day
everything
nothing
stays
things

Unit 3.2
any
enough
ever
every
own
sure
were

Unit 3.3
away
car
friends
house
our
school
very

Unit 3.4
afraid
again
few
how
read
soon

Unit 3.5
done
know
push
visit
wait

Unit 3.6
before
does
good-bye
oh
right
won't

Unit 4.1
about
enjoy
gives
surprise
worry
would

Unit 4.2
colors
draw
drew
great
over
show
sign

Unit 4.3
found

mouth
once
took
wild

Unit 4.4
above
eight
laugh
moon
touch

Unit 4.5
picture
remember
room
stood
thought

Unit 4.6
across
because
dance
only
opened
shoes
told

Unit 5.1
along
behind
eyes
never
pulling

toward

Unit 5.2
door
loved
should
wood

Unit 5.3
among
another
instead
none

Unit 5.4
against
goes
heavy
kinds
today

Unit 5.5
built
early
learn
science
through

Unit 5.6
answered
carry
different
poor